The Lion, the Witch and the Wardrobe

L-I-T *Guide*
Literature In Teaching

By C. S. Lewis

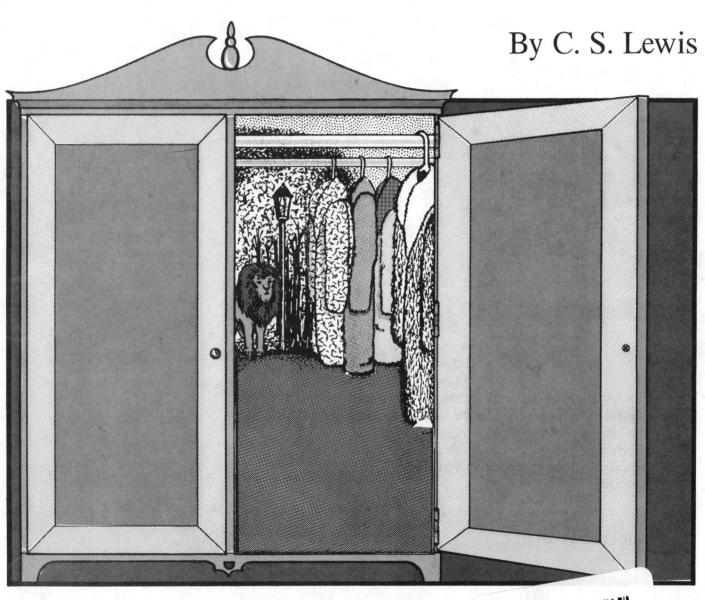

A Study Guide for Grades 4 t

Prepared by Charlotte S. Jaffe and Barba

Illustrated by Karen Sigler

The purchase of this book entitles the individual teacher to reproduce copies of the student pages for use in his or her classroom exclusively. The reproduction of any part of the work for an entire school or school system or for commercial use is prohibited.

ISBN 1-56644-006-8

EDUCATIONAL IMPRESSIONS, INC.
Hawthorne, NJ 07507

The Lion, the Witch and the Wardrobe
Written by C.S. Lewis

STORY SUMMARY

During World War II, London was subject to devastating bombing attacks. This is the story of four children—Peter, Susan, Edmund and Lucy—who are sent by their parents to the country home of a ''shaggy'' old professor in order to ensure their safety during these air raids.

While staying in the mysterious house without their parents, the children discover a fantastic land called Narnia. In this magical country they share many exciting adventures with several of the Narnians, including the tyrannical and evil White Witch; Mr. Tumnus, the friendly faun; Mr. and Mrs. Beaver; and Aslan, the brave and wonderful lion.

As among most brothers and sisters, there is both rivalry and love. When threatened, however, the love and loyalty surface. When Edmund falls under the spell of the White Witch, the others must rescue him at great peril to themselves. Edmund finally redeems himself and helps to eliminate the evil in the land of Narnia.

Meet the Author
Clive Staples Lewis

C.S. Lewis once said, "I wrote the books I should have liked to read. That's always been my reason for writing."

The renowned British author was born in Belfast, Ireland, in November 1898. His father was a lawyer, and his mathematically-talented mother was the daughter of a clergyman. They provided an enriching environment for Clive and his older brother. The two boys spent many childhood hours together drawing imaginative pictures. While his brother sketched ships, trains and battles, Clive concentrated on creating his own country, which he called "Animal Land." At the age of seven or eight, Clive began writing stories to accompany his illustrations. His first works were about chivalrous mice and rabbits. There was also a plentiful supply of books around their home. "In the seemingly endless rainy afternoons, I took volume after volume from the shelves," he said.

Sadly, Clive was only nine years old when his mother died. At first he was educated at home with tutors. Later on he was sent to private boarding schools. He attended Oxford University, but his education there was interrupted by his service in the British Army. After being wounded in France, Lewis returned to Oxford to complete his studies.

C.S. Lewis became a theologian of the Anglican Church and authored many scholarly and imaginative works of literature for adults. It was not until 1950 that he published his most famous children's book, *The Lion, the Witch and the Wardrobe*. "I am astonished how some very young children seem to understand it. I think it frightens some adults, but very few children," he said about the book. Lewis's religious views can be seen in the Christ-like role of Aslan, who dies to save Edmund on the Stone Table and then rises again. He went on to create other books about Narnia; however, he said that when he first wrote *The Lion, the Witch and the Wardrobe,* he had no notion of writing the others.

"In a certain sense," wrote Lewis, "I have never actually made a story. I see pictures. Some of these pictures have a common flavor which groups them together. Images always come first."

C.S. Lewis died in November 1963.

Pre-Reading Activities

Complete these activities before you read the book. Meet in small cooperative groups to compare answers. Share your group's responses with the entire class.

The London Blitz

During World War II, the Germans launched devastating air raids on London, England. These raids, which took place nearly every evening from September 1940 through May 1941, were called the Blitz, or the London Blitz. The British citizens steadfastly refused to negotiate with Hitler and showed great courage in withstanding the vicious attacks. However, in order to protect their children from the constant bombings, some families sent their youngsters to the safer countryside that surrounded the city.

Activity: Gather reference information about this historical event. Ask family members for their recollections about the Battle of Britain.

Mythology

The fascinating world of mythology is carefully integrated into this story. Mythological creatures used as story characters include the fauns, the dryads, the naiads, the nymphs, the centaurs, the unicorns, the satyrs, and the giants.

Activity: Locate or sketch pictures of these creatures. Read about them in mythology books and learn their origins and characteristics.

Wardrobes

Because the tax assessors counted closets as rooms, older European homes were usually built without closets. Instead, people kept their clothing in tall cabinets with doors. In England these cabinets are called wardrobes; in France they are called armoires and are usually more ornate.

Activity: Collect pictures of various types of wardrobes from magazines. Draw a picture of the kind of wardrobe you think was used in the story of *The Lion, the Witch and the Wardrobe.*

Learning British English

English is spoken as the principal language in many countries around the world. Australia, England, Ireland, Canada, Scotland, New Zealand and the United States all share the language; however, words within the language are often given different meanings, pronunciations and/or spellings. Because *The Lion, the Witch and the Wardrobe* was written by a British author, American readers will encounter many differences from their own everyday language.

Spellings
Write the American English spelling for each of the following words:

armour:

harbour:

colour:

centre:

realised:

favourite:

honour:

apologise:

Meanings
Write the American English meaning for each of the following words or expressions:

old chap:

wireless:

gum boots:

having a row:

lay the table:

larder:

batty:

sledge:

Make a list of other British English words and expressions that you find in the story. Discuss their meanings and spellings with your classmates. Then create a class bulletin board of British English words. Match them with American words and their meanings.

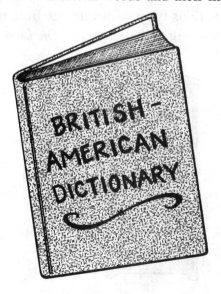

Vocabulary

Chapters One, Two and Three:
Lucy Looks into a Wardrobe, What Lucy Found There and *Edmund and the Wardrobe*

Use the words in the box to complete the sentences below. You may need to use your dictionary.

spiteful	dryad	enormous	jollification
grumbling	stole	lulling	batty
inquisitive	melancholy	parcel	row
presently	hoax	gilded	sulked
heather	groped	chap	vanish

1. "I'll be ready to leave _____," replied Joe as he put on his coat.

2. "Don't be so nosey," Erin said to her _____ sister.

3. Peg loved to explore the woods; her mom called her a _____.

4. Grandma was an expert at _____ the children to sleep.

5. The _____ was delivered by truck.

6. We knew by his constant _____ that Dad was in a bad mood.

7. She _____ in and out of the room without being noticed.

8. Because of her _____ mood, Sarah was not fun to be with today.

9. After their _____, the brothers were quick to apologize to one another.

10. It was such an _____ fish that it almost broke Mike's line and pole.

11. The thief tried to swindle me, but I knew the scheme was a _____.

12. She bought gold slippers to match her _____ robe.

13. The moody child often _____ in his room.

14. In the distance she could see the purplish flowers of the _____.

15. Still half asleep, he _____ for the telephone.

16. Everyone was laughing and having fun; he had never seen such _____.

17. The man's behavior was very strange; the others thought he was _____.

18. The _____ boy purposely spilled milk on his sister's homework.

19. Watching the sunset, the child saw the sun _____ behind the mountains.

20. Mr. Smith thought that his new neighbor seemed like a pleasant _____.

Comprehension and Discussion Questions
Chapters One, Two and Three

Answer the following questions in complete sentence form. Give examples from the story to support your response.

CHAPTER ONE: *Lucy Looks into a Wardrobe*

1. Why are Lucy, Edmund, Susan and Peter living with the Professor instead of with their parents? How would you feel if you were sent to live away from home?

_____

_____

_____

_____

2. How does Lucy's love of fur lead her to the meeting with the faun?

_____

_____

_____

_____

3. How does Lucy feel when she first enters Narnia? Is she afraid she will not be able to get back to her brothers and sisters? Explain.

_____

_____

_____

_____

CHAPTER TWO: *What Lucy Found There*

1. Why does Mr. Tumnus ask Lucy if she is a Daughter of Eve? What does he mean by this?

_____

_____

_____

_____

2. Why does Mr. Tumnus begin crying after feeding and entertaining Lucy so well?

_____

_____

_____

_____

3. What spell has the White Witch put on Narnia?

_____

_____

_____

_____

CHAPTER THREE: *Edmund and the Wardrobe*

1. What do the elder children think of Lucy's story? Why does Lucy go into the wardrobe the second time?

_____

_____

_____

_____

2. Why does Edmund follow Lucy into the wardrobe? What is his real reason for apologizing to her?

_____

_____

_____

_____

3. Whom does Edmund meet while looking for Lucy? How does she introduce herself?

_____

_____

_____

_____

Vocabulary
Chapters Four, Five and Six: *Turkish Delight*
Back on This Side of the Door and *Into the Forest*

Alphabetize the words and phrases in the vocabulary box. Then use your dictionary to define them.

fraternise	alighted	mantle	enchanted
snigger	fetch	assume	chatelaine
superior	courtier	treason	disposal
camphor	by Jove	dominion	wretched
briskly	beastly	resumed	larder

You'll Never Believe What Happened!

Imagine that you are Lucy. Write a letter to a friend describing your experience in the wardrobe. Use at least ten of the vocabulary words from the first part of this activity in your letter.

Comprehension and Discussion Questions
Chapters Four, Five and Six

Answer the following questions in complete sentence form. Give examples from the story to support your response.

CHAPTER FOUR: *Turkish Delight*

1. The White Witch succeeds in finding out many facts from Edmund. What are they? What is of particular interest to her?

_____

_____

_____

_____

2. Draw up a contract that represents the deal made between Edmund and the White Witch.

_____

_____

_____

_____

3. From Edmund's point of view, explain why it might not be fun if he tells the others that he, too, has been in Narnia.

_____

_____

_____

_____

CHAPTER FIVE: *Back on This Side of the Door*

1. Why do Peter and Susan decide to approach the Professor about Lucy's story? How does Edmund's behavior influence their decision?

_____

_____

_____

_____

2. Judge the advice the Professor gives to Peter and Susan.

_____

_____

_____

3. Explain why Peter exclaims, "Sharp's the word!" and what he means by this expression.

_____

_____

_____

_____

CHAPTER SIX: *Into the Forest*

1. Create a syllogism Susan might use to rationalize that it is all right to wear the fur coats that are in the wardrobe.

_____

_____

_____

_____

2. Edmund gives away his secret about having been in Narnia once before. Find the statement that gives him away.

_____

_____

_____

_____

3. Why is Peter so willing to follow the robin through the woods? What bothers Edmund about this course of action?

_____

_____

_____

_____

Vocabulary
Chapters Seven and Eight:
A Day with the Beavers and *What Happened After Dinner*

Read each clue and find the answers in the box. Then use the letters above the numbered spaces to decipher the secret message.

marmalade	decoy	vanished	betray	peddlars
prophecy	stratagem	sensation	token	whisked	trifle
treacherous	festoons	beckoned	boughs	dodge	gloomy

1. plan; tactics

    __ __ __ __ __ __ __ __ __
     7   18

2. jelly with rind and fruit

    __ __ __ __ __ __ __ __ __
     4   3 22

3. prediction

    __ __ __ __ __ __ __ __
     13   9

4. feeling

    __ __ __ __ __ __ __ __ __
     2   20   21

5. dangerous

    __ __ __ __ __ __ __ __ __ __ __
       1   10

6. decorative chains

    __ __ __ __ __ __ __ __
    16   5

7. object used to entice; bait

    __ __ __ __ __
       15

8. to violate a trust

    __ __ __ __ __ __
    12 19

9. branches

    __ __ __ __ __ __
    15   11

10. something of little importance

    __ __ __ __ __ __
    8 6

11. something that identifies

    __ __ __ __ __
    14   17

1 2 3 4 5   6 7   8 9 10

__ __ __ __ __   __ __   __ __ __

11 12 13 14   15 16   17 18 19 20 21 22

__ __ __ __   __ __   __ __ __ __ __ __ .

Comprehension and Discussion Questions
Chapter Seven: *A Day with the Beavers*

Answer the following questions in complete sentence form. Give examples from the story to support your response.

1. Why does the Beaver warn the children to be quiet?

_____

_____

_____

_____

2. How does Mr. Beaver prove to the children that he can be trusted?

_____

_____

_____

_____

3. Describe how each of the four children reacts when Aslan's name is mentioned for the first time.

_____

_____

_____

_____

4. As the children approach the Beavers' dam, Edmund notices something that the others do not. What does he notice?

_____

_____

_____

_____

Comprehension and Discussion Questions
Chapter Eight: *What Happened After Dinner*

1. Why does the Witch like to call herself human? What is Mr. Beaver's view of humans and of beings that appear human, but are not?

_____

_____

_____

_____

2. Explain the prophecy of the four thrones at Cair Paravel.

_____

_____

_____

_____

3. Why is Mr. Beaver sure that Edmund has gone to the home of the White Witch?

_____

_____

_____

_____

4. Why is it important to figure out exactly how long Edmund has been gone?

_____

_____

_____

_____

Vocabulary
Chapters Nine and Ten:
In the Witch's House and *The Spell Begins to Break*

Use the words in the box to complete the sentences below. You may need to use your dictionary.

spectacles	gloomy	solemn	bristling
sorcerer	turret	cordial	gloating
stammered	bundled	brambles	flask
sluice	ventured	threshold	reckoned

1. The _____ on the castle was visible in the distance.

2. He _____ on the journey despite the dangers.

3. They opened and closed the _____ gate to regulate the flow of water.

4. He scratched himself on the thorns of the prickly _____.

5. Grandmother wore her _____ to do her needlework.

6. I gave my _____ promise to study harder for the next test.

7. The embarrassed boy nervously _____ an excuse for his error.

8. The seemingly endless rain put Sarah in a _____ mood.

9. He _____ out of the house so hastily that he forgot his briefcase.

10. After the race, the vain winner stood _____ at the finish line.

11. After dinner, Mrs. Jones sipped a _____.

12. The _____ used his magical powers to chase away the evil spirits.

Some of the vocabulary words were not used in the first part of this activity. For each unused word, write an original sentence.

_____

_____

_____

_____

Comprehension and Discussion Questions
Chapter Nine: *In the Witch's House*

Answer the following questions in complete sentence form. Give examples from the story to support your response.

1. Why does Edmund leave the Beavers' home?

_____

_____

_____

_____

2. What part of the conversation with Mr. Beaver does Edmund miss by leaving when he does?

_____

_____

_____

_____

3. What frightens Edmund when he first sees the Witch's house? What frightens him upon entering the gate to the courtyard?

_____

_____

_____

_____

4. How does the Witch react to Edward's arrival? Did you expect her to react in this manner? Why or why not?

_____

_____

_____

_____

Comprehension and Discussion Questions
Chapter Ten: *The Spell Begins to Break*

1. In this chapter the Beavers and the children realize that the Witch is probably on her way. How does Mrs. Beaver's behavior differ from that of the others?

_____

_____

_____

_____

2. Why does Mr. Beaver leave the cave when he hears the sound of jingling bells? Judge whether or not you think it was the wise thing to do.

_____

_____

_____

_____

3. Explain what Mr. Beaver means when he says, "This is a nasty knock for the Witch! It looks as if her power is already crumbling."

_____

_____

_____

_____

4. What gifts does Father Christmas give to the children? Why does he tell them that they are tools not toys?

_____

_____

_____

_____

Vocabulary
Chapters Eleven and Twelve:
Aslan Is Nearer and *Peter's First Battle*

Alphabetize the words in the vocabulary box. Then use your dictionary to define them.

repulsive	creaking	swish	everlasting
standard	indulgence	gluttony	councillor
celandines	bane	transparent	currant
dense	thaw	slab	pavilion
rampant	sulkily	fidgets	vermin

Vocabulary Charade Game

Divide the class into two or more teams. Create VOCABULARY CHARADE CARDS with the word on one side and the definition on the other. The game begins when a player from one team selects a card. That player then acts out the word for his or her teammates, who have two minutes to correctly guess the word and define it. Teams alternate until all players have had a chance to act out a word or until all the words have been used. Each correct answer is worth one point.

Comprehension and Discussion Questions
Chapter Eleven: *Aslan Is Nearer*

Answer the following questions in complete sentence form. Give examples from the story to support your response.

1. Why is Edmund disappointed with the way the Witch is treating him? Give examples.

_____

_____

_____

_____

2. Why is it lucky for the children and the Beavers that it snowed again?

_____

_____

_____

_____

3. What does the Queen do that makes Edmund finally feel sorry for someone other than himself?

_____

_____

_____

_____

4. Describe the changes that are occurring in Narnia. What event do these changes foretell?

_____

_____

_____

_____

Comprehension and Discussion Questions
Chapter Twelve: *Peter's First Battle*

Answer the following questions in complete sentence form. Give examples from the story to support your response.

1. Explain how Aslan is perceived as both good and terrible by the children. Think of something that you perceive as both good and terrible.

_____

_____

_____

_____

2. How do Susan and Peter make use of the gifts given to them by Father Christmas?

_____

_____

_____

_____

3. Evaluate Peter's behavior when he sees Susan and the wolf? Do you think he acts bravely?

_____

_____

_____

_____

4. Aslan knights Peter Sir Peter Fenris-Bane. Explain the significance of this new title.

_____

_____

_____

_____

Vocabulary
Chapters Thirteen and Fourteen:
Deep Magic from the Dawn of Time
and *The Triumph of the Witch*

Part One: Choose the word in each set that is **most unlike** the first word in meaning.

1. **encamp:** travel   hike   vacate   inhabit

2. **traitor:** caretaker   tyrant   betrayer   loyalist

3. **enrage:** charm   anger   tease   enliven

4. **earnestly:** seriously   quickly   eagerly   insincerely

5. **dismay:** trouble   disguise   hope   impatience

6. **surged:** swelled   ebbed   surfaced   increased

7. **siege:** retake   attack   revolt   retreat

8. **quivering:** sickly   shakily   steady   silly

Part Two: Choose the word in each set that is **most like** the first word in meaning.

1. **thicket:** flowers   shrubs   weeds   vines

2. **sceptre:** rod   crown   throne   scroll

3. **renounce:** repeat   redo   reject   retell

4. **assaulting:** feeding   following   testing   attacking

5. **gibber:** cry   eat   obtain   chatter

6. **despair:** happiness   anger   hopelessness   desire

7. **fulfill:** adjust   complete   flatter   collect

8. **overshadow:** dominate   overturn   outburst   overrun

Choose two words from each part. Write original sentences for each.

_____

_____

_____

_____

Comprehension and Discussion Questions
Chapter Thirteen: *Deep Magic from the Dawn of Time*

Answer the following questions in complete sentence form. Give examples from the story to support your response.

1. The Witch says to the Wolf, "Be off quickly; I have a little thing to finish here while you are away." What is the "little thing" to which she is referring?

_____

_____

_____

_____

2. Describe Edmund's rescue. What goes wrong?

_____

_____

_____

_____

3. Why, do you think, does Aslan say, "Here is your brother, and—there is no need to talk to him about what is past"?

_____

_____

_____

_____

4. Use the Deep Magic to explain why the Witch believes she is owed Edmund's life.

_____

_____

_____

_____

Comprehension and Discussion Questions
Chapter Fourteen: *The Triumph of the Witch*

Answer the following questions in complete sentence form. Give examples from the story to support your response.

1. Why does Aslan give Peter instructions for the battle yet to come? What makes Peter suspect that Aslan might not be with him during the battle?

_____

_____

_____

_____

2. Describe Aslan's mood during the last part of his journey with Susan and Lucy.

_____

_____

_____

_____

3. Why does the Witch call Aslan a fool just before she kills him with the stone knife?

_____

_____

_____

_____

4. **Foreshadowing** is a way that an author prepares the reader for something that is about to happen. Did you suspect before the end of the chapter that something awful would happen to Aslan? Did you suspect that he would be killed? Find the clues that helped you figure out what would happen.

_____

_____

_____

_____

Vocabulary
Chapters Fifteen, Sixteen and Seventeen:
Deeper Magic from Before the Dawn of Time,
What Happened about the Statues
and *The Hunting of the White Stag*

Alphabetize the words in the vocabulary box. Then use your dictionary to define them.

whimpering	concealed	giddy	gorse
slacking	extraordinary	pounced	rubble
alliance	ransacking	fortress	liberated
fusty	saccharine	desperately	precious
amidst	foreboding	skirling	whisked
muzzle	gnawed	incantation	crouched

Create a Fantasy Land

C.S. Lewis created the fantasy world of Narnia. In this activity, you are to create your own fantasy land. Describe the life forms that inhabit the land. Are these life forms greatly different or only slightly different from those in your real world? What unusual powers will you give to the plants and animals? Use at least ten vocabulary words from the first part of this activity in your description.

Sketch your fantasy land. Include some of the beings that live there.

© **Educational Impressions, Inc.**

Comprehension and Discussion Questions
Chapters Fifteen, Sixteen and Seventeen

Answer the following questions in complete sentence form. Give examples from the story to support your response.

CHAPTER FIFTEEN: *Deeper Magic from before the Dawn of Time*

1. Why are Lucy and Susan in "terrible danger" for a few moments? Why don't they care?

_____

_____

_____

_____

2. What do the mice do for Aslan?

_____

_____

_____

_____

3. Explain the Deeper Magic of which the Witch has no knowledge.

_____

_____

_____

_____

CHAPTER SIXTEEN: *What Happened About the Statues*

1. How does Aslan bring the statues back to life? Describe the changed mood in the courtyard. Give specific examples. What happens that makes Lucy jump for joy?

_____

_____

_____

_____

2. What does Lucy really mean when she asks if it's safe to bring the Giant to life? What does Aslan think she means? How does Giant Rumblebuffin help them get past the gates?

_____

_____

_____

_____

3. Why is the other lion "the most pleased of the lot"? What does this tell you about Aslan?

_____

_____

_____

_____

CHAPTER SEVENTEEN: *Hunting of the White Stag*

1. Describe how Edmund has changed. Do you believe that in real life people can change? Judge whether or not Edmund should have been told about Aslan's pact with the Witch.

_____

_____

_____

_____

2. When the four children (now kings and queens) follow the White Stag into the thicket, they find a "pillar of iron with a lantern set on the top thereof." King Edmund says, "It runs in my mind that I have seen the like before; as if it were a dream, or in the dream of a dream." Why is it familiar to him?

_____

_____

_____

_____

3. In the last two paragraphs, the author gives his readers some hints regarding the Professor. What do you think you would learn about the Professor if you read the sequels to this book?

_____

_____

_____

_____

Spotlight Literary Skill
Characterization

Characterization is the method used by an author to give readers information about a character. The author tries to show the character's strengths, weaknesses and other qualities. In Chapter Eight of *The Lion, the Witch and the Wardrobe,* the children and Mr. and Mrs. Beaver discover that Edmund is missing. Fill out the following Missing Person's Report in order to help them locate him.

MISSING PERSON POLICE REPORT

CHARACTER PROFILE

Name of Missing Person:

Last Known Address:

Physical Description:

Personality Traits:

Unusual Behavior:

Suggested Cause of Disappearance:

Possible Wherabouts:

Other Pertinent Information:

MUG SHOT
(Sketch a Picture of the Missing Person)

Spotlight Literary Skill
Symbolism

A **symbol** is something that stands for a larger or more complex object or idea. Often, it is the use of a concrete thing to represent an idea or concept that cannot itself be shown visually. Here are a few symbols:

Poison/Danger   *Recycle*   *Peace*

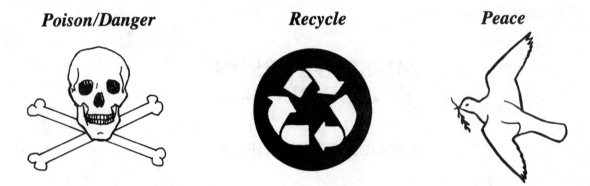

Think of at least three other symbols. Draw and label them.

In literature, the practice of using objects, events or relationships to represent other things or ideas is called **symbolism.** In *The Lion, the Witch and the Wardrobe* characters and even seasons are symbolic of concepts, ideas and values. Think about what each of the following represents in the story. Try to think of several answers. Include your reasoning.

Aslan: _____

_____

The White Witch: _____

_____

Winter: _____

_____

Spring: _____

_____

Is there another character, event or object which you feel is used symbolically? What is it and what does it represent? You might consider the following: the wardrobe, the Professor, Mrs. Macready, Mr. Tumnus, and Edmund.

Spotlight Literary Skill
Plot

A **plot** is a sequence of events that tells a story. You have just read *The Lion, the Witch and the Wardrobe*. Put the following story events in the order as they occurred in the plot. Number the events from 1 to 12.

____ The children are entertained by the Beavers.

____ Aslan brings the statues to life.

____ Father Christmas arrives in Narnia.

____ Peter and Susan ask the Professor for advice regarding Lucy's story.

____ Lucy wanders through the wardrobe into Narnia.

____ Edmund and Aslan take a walk in the dewy grass and have a conversation.

____ The Witch tempts Edmund with Turkish Delight candy.

____ The children become kings and queens.

____ Lucy meets the Faun.

____ Susan, Peter and Lucy ask Aslan to help them save Edmund.

____ The children explore the Professor's rambling country home.

____ The Witch describes Deep Magic.

Cooperative Learning Activity
Poetry from the Land of Narnia

In *The Lion, the Witch and the Wardrobe* Mr. Beaver quotes an old rhyme to acquaint the children with Aslan's powers:

> Wrong will be right, when Aslan comes in sight,
> At the sound of his roar, sorrows will be no more,
> When he bares his teeth, winter meets its death,
> And when he shakes his mane, we shall have spring again.

Along with the members of your cooperative learning group, create one or more rhymes that future Narnians might chant. Use your favorite rhyming pattern. When the poems are completed, share them orally with your entire class. Place the poems in a scrapbook entitled "Poetry from the Land of Narnia."

Crossword Puzzle
The Lion, the Witch and the Wardrobe

See how much you remember about *The Lion, the Witch and the Wardrobe*. Have fun!

Across

1. The spell prevented this holiday from being cele-brated in Narnia.
6. Father Christmas gave her a dagger.
8. The children were sent to the country because of this.
9. Type of story this is.
13. Country in which this novel takes place.
14. What 22 down is.
15. Edmund or Peter at end of story.
16. They helped Aslan by gnawing through the ropes.
18. She put a spell on Narnia.
21. He lied about having been in Narnia.
25. Father Christmas gave him a sword.
27. Accompanied the White Witch when Edmund first met her.
29. The children went to live with him.
31. Human boys were called Sons of ____.
32. Candy that tempted Edmund.
33. What Tumnis is.
34. Lucy's love of this caused her to enter the wardrobe.
35. The wicked witch turned living beings into this.

Down

2. Father Christmas gave Susan an ivory one.
3. The children were sent to the country so they would be ____.
4. The children followed a white one into the thicket in the final chapter.
5. What the "C" stands for in the author's name.
7. Author of *The Lion, the Witch and the Wardrobe*.
8. A tall cabinet designed to hold clothes.
10. Magical land discovered by the children.
11. Sequence of events in a story.
12. Season in Narnia while under the spell.
17. Human girls are called Daughters of ____.
19. What Mr. Beaver gave to the children to prove he could be trusted.
20. He broke the witch's wand.
22. Chief of the White Witch's Secret Police.
23. Lucy or Susan at end of story.
24. There were four thrones there.
26. Freed Narnia from the spell.
28. The children had been sent away from this city.
30. What 26 down is.

Post-Reading Activities

1. Divide the class into small cooperative learning groups. Each group will choose a chapter or section of the story to dramatize. Involvement may be basic or complex depending upon the interests and ability levels of the students.

2. Create a board game based upon *The Lion, the Witch and the Wardrobe.* Include a clear set of directions. Play the game with your classmates.

3. *The Lion, the Witch and the Wardrobe* is the first of seven books in C.S. Lewis's *The Chronicles of Narnia.* Read one of the sequels: *Prince Caspian, The Voyage of the "Dawn Treader," The Silver Chair, The Horse and His Boy, The Magician's Nephew* or *The Last Battle.* Compare and contrast it with *The Lion, the Witch and the Wardrobe.*

4. Based upon the descriptions in the story, draw your own interpretations of the following: the Professor, Mrs. Macready, the White Witch, and the Beavers' home.

5. Rivalry—even when there is a strong love—is not uncommon between brothers and sisters. Share an experience of a rivalry between you and a brother or a sister (or between two other siblings). Choose an experience that will not embarrass or hurt anyone.

6. Although they knew her to be a truthful girl, the others did not believe Lucy's story about the wardrobe, and Lucy felt very hurt. Have you ever had an experience in which you (or someone you know) were not believed because the truth was so odd? If so, tell about it.

7. Create a story map detailing the children's journey. Begin in the wardrobe of the Professor's mysterious house, continue through the land of Narnia, and end back in the wardrobe. Use symbols or pictures to represent the important places that they pass along the way. Be sure to label each stop! Compare your story map with those of your classmates.

Glossary of Literary Terms

Alliteration: A repetition of initial, or beginning, sounds in two or more consecutive or neighboring words.

Analogy: A comparison based upon the resemblance in some particular ways between things that are otherwise unlike.

Anecdote: A short account of an interesting, amusing or biographical occurrence.

Anticlimax: An event that is less important than what occurred before it.

Archaic language: Language that was once common in a particular historic period but which is no longer commonly used.

Cause and effect: The relationship in which one condition brings about another condition as a direct result. The result, or consequence, is called the effect.

Character development: The ways in which the author shows how a character changes as the story proceeds.

Characterization: The method used by the author to give readers information about a character; a description or representation of a person's qualities or peculiarities.

Classify: To arrange according to a category or trait.

Climax: The moment when the action in a story reaches its greatest conflict.

Compare and contrast: To examine the likenesses and differences of two people, ideas or things. (*Contrast* always emphasizes differences. *Compare* may focus on likenesses alone or on likenesses and differences.)

Conflict: The main source of drama and tension in a literary work; the discord between persons or forces that brings about dramatic action.

Connotation: Something suggested or implied, not actually stated.

Description: An account that gives the reader a mental image or picture of something.

Dialect: A form of language used in a certain geographic region; it is distinguished from the standard form of the language by pronunciation, grammar and/or vocabulary.

Dialogue (dialog): The parts of a literary work that represent conversation.

Fact: A piece of information that can be proven or verified.

Figurative language: Description of one thing in terms usually used for something else. Simile and metaphor are examples of figurative language.

Flashback: The insertion of an earlier event into the normal chronological sequence of a narrative.

Foreshadowing: The use of clues to give readers a hint of events that will occur later on.

Historical fiction: Fiction represented in a setting true to the history of the time in which the story takes place.

Imagery: Language that appeals to the senses; the use of figures of speech or vivid descriptions to produce mental images.

Irony: The use of words to express the opposite of their literal meaning.

Legend: A story handed down from earlier times; its truth is popularly accepted but cannot be verified.

Limerick: A humorous five-lined poem with a specific form: aabba. Lines 1, 2 and 5 are longer than lines 3 and 4.

Metaphor: A figure of speech that compares two unlike things without the use of like or as.

Mood: The feeling that the author creates for the reader.

Motivation: The reasons for the behavior of a character.

Narrative: The type of writing that tells a story.

Narrator: The character who tells the story.

Opinion: A personal point of view or belief.

Parody: Writing that ridicules or imitates something more serious.

Personification: A figure of speech in which an inanimate object or an abstract idea is given human characteristics.

Play: A literary work that is written in dialogue form and that is usually performed before an audience.

Plot: The arrangement or sequence of events in a story.

Point of view: The perspective from which a story is told.

Protagonist: The main character.

Pun: A play on words that are similar in sound but different in meaning.

Realistic fiction: True-to-life fiction; the people, places and happenings are similar to those in real life.

Resolution: The part of the plot from the climax to the ending where the main dramatic conflict is worked out.

Satire: A literary work that pokes fun at individual or societal weaknesses.

Sequencing: The placement of story elements in the order of their occurrence.

Setting: The time and place in which the story occurs.

Simile: A figure of speech that uses *like* or *as* to compare two unlike things.

Stereotype: A character whose personality traits represent a group rather than an individual.

Suspense: Quality that causes readers to wonder what will happen next.

Symbolism: The use of a thing, character, object or idea to represent something else.

Synonyms: Words that are very similar in meaning.

Tall tale: An exaggerated story detailing unbelievable events.

Theme: The main idea of a literary work; the message the author wants to communicate, sometimes expressed as a generalization about life.

Tone: The quality or feeling conveyed by the work; the author's style or manner of expression.

ANSWERS

Chapters One, Two and Three: Vocabulary

1. presently	5. parcel	9. row	13. sulked	17. batty
2. inquisitive	6. grumbling	10. enormous	14. heather	18. spiteful
3. dryad	7. stole	11. hoax	15. groped	19. vanish
4. lulling	8. melancholy	12. gilded	16. jollification	20. chap

Chapter One: Comprehension and Discussion Questions (Answers may vary.)

1. Like many upper- and middle-class children of the time, these children have been sent to the country to escape the bombing of London during WWII.

2. Lucy steps into the wardrobe to touch the soft, luxurious furs that are hanging there. She steps further and further in, thinking that the wardrobe is incredibly large and soon finds herself in Narnia, where she meets Mr. Tumnus.

3. Lucy feels frightened, but she is also curious and excited. She believes she can return to her brothers and sister because she can still see through the open door of the wardrobe.

Chapter Two: Comprehension and Discussion Questions (Answers may vary.)

1. Those in Narnia refer to human boys as the Sons of Adam and human girls as the Daughters of Eve. It is a reference to the biblical story of Adam and Eve as the first 2 human beings. The White Witch has ordered Tumnus to capture and turn over to her any humans he might meet.

2. He is ashamed of being in the Witch's service. ''My father would never have. . .taken service under the White Witch.'' Also, although he will not turn Lucy over to the Witch, he fears that the Witch will find out and turn him into stone.

3. She has made it always winter but never Christmas.

Chapter Three: Comprehension and Discussion Questions (Answers may vary.)

1. They do not believe her story. When they look in the wardrobe, they see nothing unusual. Also, she has been gone only a few seconds. They think she is making it up. She goes into the wardrobe a second time because she begins to wonder if the whole thing has been a dream.

2. He goes in so that he can continue to tease her about her imaginary country. He says he is sorry because he doesn't want to be alone in such a strange place.

3. Edmund meets the White Witch, who calls herself the Queen of Narnia. She is riding her sled of reindeer and is accompanied by a dwarf. She asks Edmund what he is.

Chapter Four: Comprehension and Discussion Questions (Answers may vary.)

1. She learns that he is human, that he has come into Narnia through a magic door, that he has 2 sisters and a brother, and that one of his sisters has been in Narnia and has met a Faun. She also learns that no one but he and his siblings know about Narnia. She is especially interested in the fact that there are four of them.

2. She gives him enchanted Turkish Delight (candy), a hot magic drink, and a promise to make him Prince and later on King. He promises to bring his siblings to her in secret.

3. It won't be as much fun for him because he will have to admit Lucy was right. Also, he realizes that the woman who gave him the candy was the Witch. He believes the others will side with Lucy and the Fauns; by accepting the gifts, he is already half way on the side of the Witch. He is afraid he won't be able to keep the Witch's secret once they start talking about Narnia.

Chapter Five: Comprehension and Discussion Questions (Answers may vary.)

1. Lucy thinks Edmund will back up her story. When he lies and says they have been pretending, Lucy feels betrayed. She rushes out of the room and they later see that she has been crying. When she sticks to her story, they begin to think that she is mentally ill. They tell the Professor what Lucy has told them and ask his advice.

2. The Professor points out that there are 3 logical solutions: Lucy is lying; Lucy is going insane; and Lucy is telling the truth. He says that it is obvious that she isn't mad; therefore, she is either lying or telling the truth. Because the children have said that Lucy is usually more truthful than Edmund, the Professor says to assume that her story is true and suggests that they mind their own business.

3. Lucy and Susan warn the boys that ''the Macready and a whole gang'' are coming. Peter wants to avoid seeing them. He shouts ''Sharp's the word!'' meaning that they should act quickly, or sharply, and get out of sight.

Chapter Six: Comprehension and Discussion Questions (Answers may vary.)

1. A syllogism is a form of deductive reasoning. It consists of a major premise, a minor premise and a conclusion. A possible syllogism would be the following:

A. If the coats are left in the wardrobe, they should not be considered stolen.

B. The whole country of Narnia is in the wardrobe.

C. Therefore, the coats (which are taken to Narnia) should not be considered stolen.

2. "Oughtn't we be bearing a bit more to the left, that is, it we are aiming for the lamp post."

3. Peter has been conditioned to think of robins as good. "They're good birds in all the stories I've ever read. I'm sure a robin wouldn't be on the wrong side." Edmund points out that it might be a trap. He says they can't be sure which side is right.

Chapters Seven and Eight: Vocabulary

1. stratagem   2. marmalade   3. prophecy   4. sensation   5. treacherous
6. festoons   7. decoy   8. betray   9. boughs   10. trifle   11. token
ASLAN IS THE HERO OF NARNIA.

Chapter Seven: Comprehension and Discussion Questions (Answers may vary.)

1. He is afraid the trees will hear. Most of the trees are good, but some would betray them to the Witch.

2. Mr. Beaver has the handkerchief that Lucy gave to Mr. Tumnus. He presents it as a token of his friendship with Tumnus and his allegiance to the forces of good against the White Witch.

3. Edmund feels a sensation of mysterious horror. Peter feels brave and adventurous. Susan feels as if a delicious smell or delightful music has floated by. Lucy feels the way one does when one wakes to find it is the beginning of the holidays or of summer.

4. He sees a small river. Looking up the valley of that river he sees 2 small hills, which he believes to be the same hills that the Witch pointed out to him.

Chapter Eight: Comprehension and Discussion Questions (Answers may vary.)

1. The Witch claims to be human because it is the basis of her claim to be Queen of Narnia. She is not really human; she is descended on one side from Adam's first wife Lilith, who was not human, and on the other side from the giants. Mr. Beaver admits that "there may be two views about Humans," but he is extremely suspicious of any being that appears to be human and isn't.

2. The prophecy states that when 2 Sons of Adam and 2 Daughters of Eve sit in the 4 thrones at Cair Paravel, the reign of the White Witch will end and she will die. The Witch fears the children will fulfill the prophecy.

3. "He had the look of one who has been with the Witch and eaten her food. You can always tell them if you've lived long in Narnia, something about their eyes."

4. "How much he can tell her depends upon how much he heard." They aren't sure if Edmund heard that the meeting place was at the Stone Table. If so, the Witch can cut them off before they meet Aslan.

Chapters Nine and Ten: Vocabulary

1. turret   2. ventured   3. sluice   4. brambles   5. spectacles   6. solemn
7. stammered   8. gloomy   9. bundled   10. gloating   11. cordial   12. sorcerer

Chapter Nine: Comprehension and Discussion Questions (Answers may vary.)

1. Edmund wants to find his way to the Witch's palace to tell her the news that his brother and sisters are near and that Aslan is coming.

2. Edmund has not heard that the Witch is not really human. He has also missed Mr. Beaver's explanation of the prophecy regarding the four thrones. (See Chapter VIII.)

3. The house's towers look like a sorcerer's caps in the moonlight. "Their long shadows looked strange on the snow!" The figure of a lion in the courtyard frightens him until he realizes it is made of stone.

4. The Witch is angry that Edmund's brother and sisters aren't with him, but "a slow cruel smile" comes over her face when she learns they are nearby. She seems shocked to learn that Aslan is in Narnia. Edmund seems surprised at her reaction to him; he expected to be treated as kindly as he had been during their last meeting.

Chapter Ten: Comprehension and Discussion Questions (Answers may vary.)

1. Rather than bolt for the door as the others do, Mrs. Beaver packs a bundle of supplies—ham, tea, sugar, utensils, handkerchiefs, etc.—for each of them. She even puts on her snow boots. Although the others are anxious to get a head start, she points out that because they are walking and the Witch has a sledge, there is little hope of them getting there first anyway. "We can't get there *before* her but we can keep under cover and go by ways she won't expect and perhaps we'll get through."

2. Mr. Beaver wants to listen to the sound of the bells to determine which way the Witch is traveling.

3. Father Christmas has arrived. This is a sign that the Witch's spell (that it will be always winter but never Christmas) is lessening.

4. He gives Peter a sword (with a sheath and belt) and a shield. Susan gets an ivory horn, a bow and a quiver full of arrows. Lucy gets a dagger and a bottle of a special cordial. Peter's gifts are signs that there will be a battle in which he will fight. The girls' gifts are to protect them from danger.

Chapter Eleven: Comprehension and Discussion Questions (Answers may vary.)

1. Edmund expects to be given Turkish Delight and to be treated well, but the Witch is cruel to him. She gives him only stale bread and water to eat and takes him on a journey without the proper clothing to keep him warm.

2. ''It would have been a dreadful thing...if the night had remained fine....The wolves would then have been able to follow their trail....Now that the snow had begun...the scent was cold and...the footprints were covered up.''

3. The Witch turns a merry party—a squirrel family, and old dog-fox, a dwarf and 2 satyrs—into stone for saying that Father Christmas had given them the things to eat and drink.

4. It is turning to spring. The snow is melting; patches of green are appearing; birds are singing; flowers are blooming. Aslan is getting closer and the Witch's spell is disappearing.

Chapter Twelve: Comprehension and Discussion Questions (Answers may vary.)

1. Aslan represents goodness. The children have placed all of their hope in him and yet they are afraid to look at him. He ''caused fear and alarm.'' One meaning of *terrible* is ''causing fear or alarm.''

2. Susan uses her horn to get help when the wolf chases her up a tree. Peter uses his sword to slay the wolf.

3. He is afraid and does not feel brave; however, he acts heroically. He does what he has to do: kill the wolf and save his sister's life.

4. Fenris is the giant wolf of Norse mythology. *Bane* means ''a cause of destruction.''

Chapters Thirteen and Fourteen: Vocabulary

PART 1: 1. vacate 2. loyalist 3. charm 4. insincerely 5. hope 6. ebbed 7. retreat 8. steady
PART 2: 1. shrubs 2. rod 3. reject 4. attacking 5. chatter 6. hopelessness 7. complete 8. dominate

Chapter Thirteen: Comprehension and Discussion Questions (Answers may vary.)

1. The ''little thing'' is the killing of Edmund. She would have preferred to kill him on the Stone Table, where killings such as this had been done before, but she fears he will be rescued.

2. While the Witch sharpens her knife, Edmund is rescued by a party of centaurs, deer, unicorns and birds. The rescue is successful, but the Witch and the Dwarf escape. The Witch has used her magic wand to change herself into a stump and the Dwarf into a boulder.

3. Edmund has seen the error of his ways; therefore, there is no longer a need to discuss it with him.

4. On the Stone Table is written an ancient law. It is also on the trunk of the World Ash Tree and on the sceptre of the Emperor-Beyond-the-Sea. It states that every traitor belongs to the Witch as her lawful prey and that for every treachery she has the right to a kill. Unless she has ''blood as the Law says all Narnia will be overturned and perish in fire and water.''

Chapter Fourteen: Comprehension and Discussion Questions (Answers may vary.)

1. Aslan knows that he will not be there to guide Peter during the battle. Peter suspects that Aslan won't be with him because of Aslan's use of the word ''you'' instead of ''we'' throughout his explanation.

2. Aslan has become sad. He does not talk much and appears not to be concentrating on what they say.

3. She thinks him a fool because she thinks she will be able to kill the children as soon as she kills Aslan.

4. In the previous chapter Aslan agreed that the Witch has a right to a kill. Aslan does not say that she has renounced this right, but only that she has renounced the claim on Edmund's blood. In this chapter he infers that he will not be with Peter during the battle. We get the feeling something awful is about to happen. ''It was as if the good times...were already drawing to their end.'' ''Either some dreadful thing that is going to happen to him, or something dreadful that he's going to do.''

Chapter Fifteen: Comprehension and Discussion Questions (Answers may vary.)

1. The Witch sends out the Spectres, Minotaurs, vultures and giant bats in search of the humans and they go right past the girls' hiding place. They are so filled with sadness caused by Aslan's death, however, that they don't think about the danger that surrounds them.

2. The mice gnaw through the ropes that bind Aslan.

3. Her knowledge goes back only to the dawn of Time. There is a different incantation from before the dawn of Time. "When a willing victim who had committed no treachery was killed in a traitor's stead, the Table would crack and Death itself would start working backwards." (There is an obvious analogy to the death and resurrection of Christ.)

Chapter Sixteen: Comprehension and Discussion Questions (Answers may vary.)

1. Aslan breathes life into the statues. The author compares what happens to the igniting of a newspaper with a match. Life creeps over their bodies until they are fully restored. The mood becomes happy. "Creatures were running after Aslan and dancing round him." "Courtyard was now a blaze of colours." "Instead of the deadly silence the whole place rang with the sounds of happy roarings...songs and laughter." Lucy jumps for joy when she finds Mr. Tumnus.

2. She wants to know if it's safe for them to have the Giant alive. Aslan thinks she wants to know if it's safe for the Giant if Aslan breathes only on his feet.

The Giant breaks the walls and gates with his club and lets the creatures out of the castle courtyard.

3. Aslan tells those with good noses to come in the front with "*us lions.*" He acts as if he is just one of the lions and not a god-like creature. He is very humble.

Chapter Seventeen: Comprehension and Discussion Questions (Answers may vary.)

1. Edmund acts both heroically and wisely as shown in his breaking of the Witch's wand. He is no longer thinking only of himself.

2. This is the same lamp-post that the Witch pointed out to him in Chapter IV—the post under which Lucy met the Faun.

3. They would learn that the Professor had been in Narnia. The fact that he believes their story and tells them not to mention it to anyone who hasn't had similar experiences is a clue to this fact. Also, he seems to know about Narnia.

Spotlight Literary Skill: Symbolism
Suggested answers are as follows:
Aslan: The Savior, Christ, Personification of Goodness
The White Witch: Personification of Evil, Satan, The Arch Enemy
Winter: Dismay, Gloom, Sorrow, Barrenness, Despair, Infertility
Spring: Hope, New Life, Rebirth

Spotlight Literary Skill: Plot
6-11-7-5-2-9-4-12-3-8-1-10

Crossword Puzzle: